LEXINGTON AND CONCORD
IN COLOR

LEXINGTON

AND CONCORD

in Color

*With an Introductory Text
and Notes on the Illustrations by*
STEWART BEACH

*A Collection of Color
Photographs by*
SAMUEL CHAMBERLAIN

HASTINGS HOUSE · PUBLISHERS
New York, 10016

PUBLISHED 1970 BY HASTINGS HOUSE, PUBLISHERS, INC.

Published simultaneously in Canada by
Saunders, of Toronto, Ltd., Don Mills, Ontario

Library of Congress Catalog Card Number: 78-119796
SBN 8038-4269-4
Printed and bound in England by Jarrold and Sons Ltd, Norwich

CONTENTS

The Dawn of Our Republic

LEXINGTON AND CONCORD came into sudden glory on April 19, 1775, when their militia companies and minutemen engaged a sizable force of British regulars in the first battles of what would become the Revolutionary War fifteen months later, in July, 1776. The glory has never faded. Thousands of tourists come each year to view the shrines where the history of our nation began. The shrines are still there—Lexington Green where the first encounter took place in the early dawn and the North Bridge in Concord which, later that morning, saw professional British soldiers put to rout by a force of Americans made up chiefly of angry farmers in arms.

Beginning in 1975 America will celebrate the bicentenary of these and other events of the Revolutionary War. We will have been two hundred years a nation and this is something indeed to celebrate. Well, these are the very places it began—in Lexington and Concord, hallowed in the memory of our past and our beginning.

After it was all over at Yorktown and peace returned to the colonies which now were states with stars on a flag, Concord had a new and notable flowering of literature. It was tied to Boston, which was not so many miles away and called itself "the Athens of America." But the center of this nineteenth-century renaissance was in Concord as much as in Boston, with giants of literature living there. The houses—most of them—are still to be seen and many are open to the public. What memories they evoke! Ralph Waldo Emerson, Nathaniel Hawthorne, Bronson Alcott and his daughter, Louisa May, who wrote *Little Women*; Henry David Thoreau, who peopled the shores of Walden Pond with a naturalist's love of wild things and developed the philosophy which made him a quiet citizen of the world. These were brilliant years, and why the chief figures came together in Concord seems to have been a matter of both choice and chance. For something like fifty years the great writers whose works became classics in their time, lived and dreamed and wrote in this pleasant town. It is something to think of when you go there and bring alive for yourself the rich reality of more than a hundred years ago.

In the span of America's life both Lexington and Concord rank as ancient towns. Concord, the older, was settled in 1634 and in 1635 was granted standing by the General Court in Boston as a new "plantation," six square miles in extent. This was but five years after the Province of Massachusetts Bay was founded in 1630 with John Winthrop as its governor. The bold and adventurous men and women who came to the site on the Concord River established themselves at a farther distance from Boston than any of the other towns which depended from the capital. Concord was some twenty miles away, and that was a considerable distance through the wilderness with no roads and no friendly farms or inns where the travelers might seek food and shelter. Still, they knew what they wanted and had soon established a town in the exact center of their six square miles.

Lexington's development was quite different from Concord's. It was a loose collection of separated farms, and for many years these were not centered upon any village. The area was part of Cambridge and known as Cambridge Farms. In 1642 the pioneers moved in, but it was a long time before they established a village. Not until 1712 did the General Court grant them status as a separate town, though by this time it was a viable community with its church and its town meeting, the two first bulwarks of American settlements in colonial times. It had no particular need to expand. By this time the farms were prosperous, and there were roads which made travel easier. The men could get into Boston when they chose, to buy the staples they could not raise. Both Lexington and Concord became small centers of agricultural communities. There was no industry in Massachusetts Bay, nor would there be until after the Revolution. Although attempts were made now and then to stimulate manufacturing the colonists showed no interest. They lived by agriculture—or by the sea. Along the seaboard a thriving shipping business was growing before the end of the seventeenth century, laying fortunes for the merchants who were already becoming wealthy through their trade with the West Indies. Soon their ships were venturing to Europe.

8

In these early years there was no open quarrel with England. The shipping merchants grumbled over customs duties, but these were rather easily evaded by open smuggling, paying off a minor official to look the other way while a valuable cargo was unloaded, or plying him with strong drink in the ship's cabin. Everything worked out quite smoothly. Of course none of the shipping activity was a concern of the farming communities.

The colonists were fiercely loyal to the King and proud to be his subjects. They spoke of England as "home," though few of them would ever go there. They called themselves "British Americans." In many ways it was simply a sentimental attachment, something remembered by the later generations from what fathers and grandfathers had told them. They knew almost nothing of what was going on in London and, until the 1760s, they gave no thought at all to the British Parliament and its powers: They were subjects of the King, their rights as free-born Englishmen secured in a royal charter granted by William and Mary in 1691. The rights were all spelled out on long sheets of parchment treasured in Boston. They had not read them, but everyone knew what they said. Very early in our history the colonists developed a deep sense of their liberties which in the end, more than any other influence, caused the separation from the mother country.

With the passing of years, both Lexington and Concord grew in self-sufficiency. They became pleasant provincial towns with shops and the taverns where a man could sit at ease and talk with his friends. Fine houses were built in the eighteenth century, some still standing, to give a flavor of the ample lives the leading families had earned through the back-breaking work of their forefathers—and themselves. Much of their agricultural produce rumbled away to Boston, the metropolis, for Boston produced almost nothing to feed itself. There was little room for farming on the small peninsula in the harbor which circumscribed the town.

Then, in 1756, began the French and Indian War, which is called abroad the Seven Years War, for English armies were also engaged with the French on the Continent. Massachusetts men volunteered heavily to go with the British regiments to Canada. Lexington alone furnished 148, an impressive number considering the size of the town's population. When the war was settled by the Treaty of Paris in 1763, the American soldiers were already back home. They were veterans now and had helped the British regulars to give the final defeat to the French empire in North America. The men from Concord and Lexington formed the nucleus of the militia companies and later of the minutemen. John Parker, captain of the Lexington militia company, had been with the force that captured the great French fortress and naval base of Louisburg on Cape Breton Island.

From the end of the French and Indian War a change came over the relations with England, though the Americans lost none of their loyalty to the King. There was a new one now, for George III had been crowned in 1760 after the death of his grandfather, George II. The King was young—twenty-two when he took the throne—a handsome youth and English born, which his two German predecessors had not been. The Americans were delighted to throw their hats in the air and cheer the young monarch.

What disturbed them were rumors coming out of England that Parliament was planning taxes on the colonists to help liquidate the war with France and pay a part of the increased cost of empire. Taxes? Parliament could not levy taxes on the Americans. Their sacred charter gave them specifically the right to tax themselves, and they did not intend to abandon it, Parliament or no Parliament. For months they were restive over the rumors, but they were rumors only, scraps of gossip brought by ships' crewmen or passengers who could have had no access to official intentions. To us who are accustomed to instant communications the world over the situation in the eighteenth century seems incredible. Yet all news had to come by sea, and the sailing vessels normally took at least two months—sometimes more—to make the passage from England to America.

Parliament's first assault on the Americans was passage of a stamp act in 1765. This required that every sort of legal transaction—wills, marriages, deaths, bills of lading, ship clearances, land sales and purchases—must be recorded on stamped paper to be bought from a stampmaster in each colony. The Americans were outraged. They simply refused to cooperate in any way with a law which they considered flagrantly illegal. The act went into effect on November 1, 1765, and all business ceased for a time. The courts closed down because the judges were apprehensive of acting without the stamped papers, and these the people refused to use. Shipping was idle: Merchants also refused to buy the papers for clearances. There were riots in Boston. Gradually the situation quieted. In mid-December ships began to clear from Boston and other ports without stamped papers. The following spring the courts reopened, and in March Parliament, convinced that the act could not be enforced, repealed it entirely. There was rejoicing when the news was received two months later in Boston.

There were other assaults from Parliament, and the Americans were bewildered by them as much as they were outraged. They had no relation to Parliament, they insisted, and they refused flatly to pay attention to the acts. The men of Lexington and Concord stood stoutly with Boston. They were close, so they knew what their leaders were thinking. But no one had any idea of what Parliament was intending until the text of its acts came over the sea, weeks after they had been passed and probably forgotten by the Members of Parliament who voted them into law.

Those days of the late 1760s and early 1770s were a time of anxiety and uncertainty in Lexington and Concord. The tranquility of the earlier years was gone. By May, 1774, the port of Boston had been closed to all shipping by the British. Was it to be battle? Well, Concord and Lexington were preparing themselves. They were ready to pledge their "lives, their fortunes, and their sacred honor," as the Declaration of Independence would announce, to preserve their liberties.

Although the battle sites at both Lexington and Concord are not much changed (except for the monuments) from the way they appeared on the fateful morning in 1775, the emotional experience of seeing them for the first time can hardly be appreciated without knowing some of the immediate history. Why did the battles happen—and how? With some background in your mind they can seem as fresh as yesterday. So now let us sketch in the background, for this day was the very dawn of our Republic.

The story begins, rightly enough, in Boston which had always been the capital of the Province of Massachusetts Bay. When you are there you must surely walk what is known as "the Freedom Trail" and comprises the eighteenth-century buildings and streets which were the heart of old Boston. You will see the Town House, now called the Old State House, where from 1713 the business of the provincial government was conducted and its legislature sat. In front of the building, marked by a tablet in the pavement, is the spot where the Boston Massacre took place on March 5, 1770.

Among other buildings there is Faneuil Hall (the pronunciation is "Fann'l"), called "the Cradle of Liberty," where the fiery town meetings were held in the years leading up to the Revolution. You will visit Paul Revere's house on North Square, the only seventeenth-century building which survives in Boston; Christ Church, better known as the Old North Church, from whose steeple the lanterns were hung to signal the watchers in Charlestown on the evening of April 18 that the British troops were being rowed across the Back Bay for a march to seize the military stores the provincials had hidden in and around Concord. Nearby is the old burying ground on Copps Hill which overlooks the place where a ferry crossed the Charles River long before a bridge was built to connect Boston with Charlestown.

Coming back you will reach Washington Street where the Old South Meeting House still stands, scene not only of Sunday worship but of turbulent town meetings, moved there from Faneuil Hall because of the church's greater capacity. From there you will climb the rise to Tremont Street which runs along the Common. To the right is King's Chapel, Anglican before the Revolution but Unitarian later, when the new theology had attracted many Bostonians at the beginning of the nineteenth century. Here are the box pews which were standard in colonial days, with low doors opening on the aisle. Here a family sat, grown-ups and children, during the two long morning and afternoon services of a Sunday. And oh, how cold they were in winter, for there was no heating, and how long the sermons were! It must have been a relief for even the most devout when the morning service was over and families could descend on a nearby tavern—and there were plenty of fine ones in eighteenth-century Boston—to thaw out in the warmth of great wood-burning fireplaces and enjoy a sumptuous meal, with Madeira for the ladies and rum concoctions for the men to fortify them for the equally long service in the afternoon.

Beside King's Chapel is its ancient burying ground with quaintly carved slate tombstones which record the last resting place of early Bostonians, their wives, and often regrettably young children. Across Tremont Street is the Old Granary Burying Ground where many of the Revolutionary leaders are interred, John Hancock and Samuel Adams among them. Though their places are marked, a nineteenth-century commissioner, disturbed by the haphazard choice of grave sites, cut paths through the cemetery and simply moved the stones to make a more orderly arrangement. It no longer matters. The bones have long since been dust, and these stones are only memorials to the great, the illustrious who were dedicated to guarding the liberties of British Americans on this far shore.

You will have been seeing visible survivals of eighteenth-century Boston, but you must know something, too, of the geography of the town in those

12

distant days, for its geography played an important part in what happened in April, 1775. You cannot trace it today, but Boston was a pear-shaped peninsula connected with the mainland only by a long and narrow natural causeway on the south known as the Neck. To the west was the Back Bay, a sheet of low tidewater, which rose and fell. On the north of Boston the Charles River helped to flush the saltwater into Boston Bay, but when the tide rose it came back.

To the east were the waters of Boston Bay, dotted with islands, and at the shore were the wharves that served the extensive shipping, the shipyards themselves, the ropewalks, the warehouses and counting houses of the wealthy merchants who were responsible for the town's prosperity as a center of seaborne trade and the metropolis of Massachusetts.

The waterfront was normally an intensely busy place but in the early summer of 1774 it suddenly went dead. As a reprisal for the cargoes of tea destroyed in the Boston Tea Party the previous December Parliament shut the port until the tea was paid for. Except for British naval vessels, no ship of any sort, not even a rowboat, was permitted to ride the waters of the harbor. The seat of government was moved to Salem, and Boston suffered in the grip of unemployment and depression. The town had always lived by its shipping. When that was cut off it had no other means of livelihood. One thing was agreed among them all: The colonists would not pay for the tea.

The act took effect on June 1. A few days before General Thomas Gage came up from New York, appointed by King George to be royal governor of the province and to teach order to what were called in England "the mobbish Bostonians." He arrived with four regiments of British soldiers at his back. When he had taken time to study the size of the problem of pacifying the countryside he realized that four regiments were not enough. By April, 1775, he had ten regiments in and around Boston with 400 marines. While this seems a considerable force—and it was on paper—the total number of his effectives was around 4,000 men. It was still not enough to do the job, Gage thought, and asked the ministry in London for 20,000. This number was never forthcoming.

Gage had spent much of his military life in America. He had come here in 1754 to serve under General Jeffrey Amherst, who was the commander-in-chief of all British forces in North America. He had married a handsome American wife. He had experience in guerrilla fighting with the Indians and was with General Braddock, as was George Washington, at the desperate ambush and defeat of Braddock's force in 1755. Most of Gage's service was in Canada, but when Amherst gave up his command in 1763 and returned to England, where he was created a baron in 1776, Gage succeeded him as commander-in-chief with headquarters in New York. He had been in Boston once before in October, 1768, after two British regiments were brought down from Halifax to curb rioting in the town. Gage was back in New York when this earlier occupation came to a sudden end after the Boston Massacre. Following the demand of an angry town meeting in the Old South Meeting House over the fatal shooting of five citizens by the soldiers in the course of a squabble before the Town House, the troops were withdrawn from Boston proper and quartered at Castle William, the island fortress in the harbor.

Gage was an excellent administrator but has been judged a man of mediocre military skill. Under different circumstances he would doubtless have been well liked by the people of Boston. He was conciliatory, thoughtful, approachable, always ready to give the citizens every break. His officers thought him far too soft under the circumstances. Behind his back they called him "Tommy" and "Old Woman," and these were not terms of endearment.

In the summer of 1774 Gage called a session of the legislature—the Great and General Court as it was, and still is, known in Massachusetts—but shortly dismissed it in alarm at its actions. To make sure they passed the measures they wanted, Samuel Adams locked the door of the hall in Salem and put the key in his pocket when he learned that one of Gage's officers was on his way with a notice that the session was summarily cut off. By the time Adams unlocked the door, every measure the assembly wanted had been passed and given legal substance. One of the acts was to appoint a delegation to represent Massachusetts Bay at the Continental Congress, the first meeting ever held of all the colonies, scheduled to convene at Philadelphia in September.

The hot summer dragged on. In August the delegation left for Philadelphia, traveling in a fine coach with two outriders in front and two behind. Boston was in a state of complete inactivity, all business halted, and there was no sign from Gage that he intended to take any action that would return the province to normalcy. The Americans were still agreed on one thing: They would never pay for the tea.

The sturdy, independent, liberty-loving citizens found the situation not only maddening but intolerable. Since 1630 the leaders of the province had guided their own affairs. Parliament, which had assumed vastly more power in England since the coming of George I in 1714 paid no attention to the royal charter. But until the closing of the port in 1774 Parliament had always backed down from its demands on Massachusetts Bay. Now, with soldiers everywhere, they gave no indication of backing down. The provincial leaders must find by themselves some way to restore their self-government.

Gage himself, without intending to, gave them the opportunity. He called a new session of the legislature for Salem on October 5. Then, with his well-known indecisiveness, on September 25 he informed the assembly that its members did not need to attend. He did not forbid the session, however, so the representatives gathered at Salem on October 5. Realizing that they could accomplish nothing under the legal structure of the royal governor, they boldly formed a Provincial Congress to meet in Concord without official authorization. John Hancock would be its president. At Salem they also appointed a Committee of Safety, to act when the Congress was not in session and keep the Congress informed of what Gage was doing.

It was easy enough to learn what Gage was doing—nothing. Paul Revere constituted himself chief of intelligence in the town and enlisted the unemployed workmen as a listening force. By lounging near the barracks and on the Common, around the fortification on the Neck, they picked up bits of gossip and information which later would prove invaluable. Gage made no public protest against the Provincial Congress. Outside of Boston and Salem he had no control over the countryside. He knew what was going on, however. His chief informant was Dr. Benjamin Church, a trusted member of the Committee of Safety. None of the Americans suspected Church's treachery. From the beginning of the trouble in 1763 he had been one of the most dedicated patriots, and no one knows now what led him to accept Gage's bounty.

Without learning Gage's plans, and he had none that autumn, the Provincial Congress authorized an army of 15,000 men. This meant a beefing up of the militia companies, and later there were formed companies of minutemen who were always to carry their muskets and be ready at "a minute's notice" to oppose the British regulars. How this force would be used the Provincial Congress had no way of knowing. They were simply preparing for any coercive move into the country that Gage might make with his regiments.

After its first meeting in October, 1774, the Provincial Congress convened again at Concord on February 10, 1775. They added up the stores of food and munitions that had been moved into Concord and hired men to make cartridges for the muskets. They approved the purchase of more cannon and mortars. Gage was worried. He ordered several practice marchouts from which his troops always returned to Boston. But on each of these maneuvers the patriots assembled so quickly and in such numbers with their muskets that he felt he must move out and take the stores in Concord. If he could seize the guns and munitions he would leave these country folk with no capability of opposing his wishes.

As April approached with a drying out of the sloughs of winter roads he made his decision. On Saturday, April 15, the grenadier and light infantry companies of each of the British regiments were relieved of regular duties "till further notice." The reasons given were "exercise and new evolutions." Revere reported this move to Dr. Joseph Warren, the only member of the Committee of Safety still in Boston, who sent word to those outside the town. Toward midnight Revere had word that the boats of the transports and men-of-war had been launched and were carried under the sterns of the vessels. His intelligence force had reported earlier that the crews were at work repairing the boats. Taken together, these two developments strongly suggested that the expected marchout was about to take place. Revere conferred with Warren again, and they decided he should ride out next day to warn Samuel Adams and John Hancock. The Provincial Congress had adjourned that day, and the two men were guests of the Reverend Jonas Clarke, the patriot minister of the church in Lexington.

After hearing Revere's news in Lexington, urgent messages were sent to Colonel James Barrett, in command of the situation in Concord, to begin moving the stores to more distant places of concealment. It is somewhat amazing how much military gear had been collected over the winter, most of it distributed among the houses in the town. Now the wagons began to roll hastily, loaded with kegs of powder, musket balls, flints, cannon and cannon balls, together with barrels of dried fish, meat and other staples to provide rations for the army if it was raised.

Revere rode back by way of Charlestown and sought out one of the prominent Sons of Liberty. Revere told him what he knew, and they agreed that a watch would be set each night. When the marchout started Revere would have one light shown in the steeple of the Old North Church if the troops were going out over the Neck—by land. If they were being ferried over the Back Bay—by sea—to take a shorter route two lanterns would be hung.

In either case a messenger would be sent immediately from Charlestown to warn Lexington and Concord what was afoot. Revere crossed over to Boston by the ferry.

The following Tuesday, April 18, it was apparent that the troops were going out. Gage planned this as a secret maneuver, and it was as little secret as most such expeditions are when they must originate in a town whose inhabitants are largely hostile. Revere's intelligence scouts knew of it early, though it was evening before they were sure the Back Bay route had been chosen. Gage gave command of the 800-man force to Lieutenant-Colonel Francis Smith. Still pursuing his illusion of secrecy, evidently Gage did not inform Smith of his assignment until very late in the afternoon or early in the evening. Two young officers who had gone into the country in disguise a month before would show Smith the roads. Gage also gave Smith a list of the stores in Concord and where they were hidden, information which Dr. Church had furnished.

After dismissing Smith, Gage called his second in command, Hugh, Earl Percy, to his residence, and informed him of the plan, though Percy would have no part in the night march. To this day it is not clear whether Gage had discussed the foray with Percy earlier. It seems incredible that he would not have done so, but Gage was a cautious man. In any case, Percy walked back to his quarters across the Common. Seeing a knot of men in conversation he approached them and listened. One man said, "The British troops have marched but they will miss their aim." Percy moved up. "What aim?" he asked. "Why, the cannon at Concord," the man answered. Percy hurried back to tell Gage what he had heard. But there was nothing to be done now. The troops were entering the boats, which had been drawn up to the foot of the Common, at that time lapped by the tidal waters of the Back Bay.

This was about nine o'clock. Shortly after, Paul Revere was summoned to the house of Dr. Warren. Warren told him that he had already dispatched William Dawes to try to get through the guard at the Neck and wanted Revere to have the signal lights shown for the watchers on the Charlestown shore. He hoped Revere could get over, too. Revere immediately went to the Old North and arranged for two lanterns to be hung. Then he strode home to North Square, pulled on his boots and took a cloak, for the wind was easterly that night, and it was chilly. He had a boat hidden near the ferry, and two friends ready to row him across. The moon, which had been full the previous Saturday, was up now and still bright. Revere was apprehensive that his boat might be stopped. It was "young flood", he wrote later, and the *Somerset*, a man-of-war anchored at the mouth of the Charles, was "winding" with the change of tide. But the rowboat was not challenged and reached the Charlestown shore. The lights had been seen and a messenger sent out.

A horse was obtained for Revere, and he rode across Charlestown Neck to confront two horsemen he identified as British officers, for Gage had sent out several parties of officers that afternoon in advance to waylay messengers who might be seeking news of the expedition. One of the men spurred at him, the other turned to cut him off. Revere wheeled his horse and took the road to Medford, escaping easily as the second officer's horse became mired in a swamp. From there he sped on without further trouble, warning houses along the way and alerting the commander of the minutemen at Medford. Presently he was back on the main road and arrived at Lexington about midnight. He was directed to Parson Clarke's house where Sergeant William Munroe, pro-prietor of the Munroe Tavern, was standing guard with a squad of militia.

William Dawes came in a half-hour later and, after telling their story, the two rode on to alarm Concord. A short way out they met Samuel Prescott, a Concord doctor, who had been calling on his sweetheart. He joined them enthusiastically, and the three rode on, rousing the houses along the way. Revere was ahead when he encountered one of Gage's officer patrols, heavily armed. Prescott jumped his horse over a fence and continued to Concord where he gave the alarm. Dawes wheeled and escaped. Revere was directed into a pasture where he spurred for a wood, only to be met by other officers.

When he was brought back to the road he told a British major that there were 500 men on Lexington Green waiting for the troops. This alarmed the officer, and his little party started back to Lexington where Revere was released. The major continued down the road, met the arriving troops, and told Colonel Smith what Revere had said. Smith found this not hard to believe, for he had heard alarm guns fired and church bells rung for the past two hours of the march. The secrecy of the expedition was obviously lost. He had already sent a messenger back to Gage asking for reinforcements.

Now Smith ordered the light-infantry companies forward to clear this hostile force, with Major Pitcairn in command. Of course Revere's statement was a wild exaggeration. When Pitcairn reached Lexington there were between sixty and seventy militiamen drawn up in two lines across the Green. John

Parker, their captain, first ordered his men to stand. Then, seeing the strength of the British, he told them to leave the field and not to fire. Pitcairn rode on the Green and ordered the Americans to lay down their arms. "Disperse, ye rebels!" is the command history says he gave.

And then what happened? Who fired first? Both sides had orders not to fire unless fired on. It seems certain that the militiamen did not start it, and such an accusation was never seriously made by the British. Platoons of light infantry were now marching on the Green. Some say that an onlooker—not a member of the militia—pulled the trigger of a musket or pistol which made "a flash in the pan," meaning that the powder in the pan of the flintlock flared up but did not drop through the hole in the breech to touch off the powder in the barrel and fire the bullet. Some say that one of the heady young officers at Pitcairn's back fired his own pistol at the dispersing militiamen. It was a tense moment, and the platoons moved forward. Without an order they fired three volleys at the Americans, leaving ten dead and eight others wounded. One old man, sitting down to reload his musket, was bayoneted. Pitcairn, who had driven his sword down as a signal to cease firing, was furious that his men had gone out of control. He re-formed their ranks hastily and ordered them to the road where they took their place in the van of the grenadiers, heading for Concord.

That is the sum of the fight on Lexington Green. It was over in a few minutes. The Americans for fifty years tried to learn from the survivors of the militia company just what happened. Did some of them fire as they were dispersing? It seems plausible after the volleys of the light infantry. But no British soldiers were killed, though two young officers were wounded, and Pitcairn's horse suffered a slight wound, perhaps inflicted by a British pistol from behind. Pitcairn stoutly denied that he had given any order to fire. He would certainly have done so if the Americans in line had started shooting at his men. From all contemporary evaluation Pitcairn was a fine and responsible officer and no hothead. Two months later he was killed at the Battle of Bunker Hill and is buried in the crypt of the Old North Church in Boston.

Concord is only a few miles from Lexington, and the column reached the town about seven o'clock. The militia and minutemen had been alerted for several hours and some time after daylight they had rumors of the Lexington engagement. Around six or six-thirty they decided to go down the road and reconnoiter. They formed a column and marched for a mile or more, fifes and drums playing. "We had grand music," one of the men recalled later. Presently they saw the British approaching, a brave show of red and white uniforms in the clear air of the crisp April morning. Some of the militia were for engaging them immediately, but cooler heads prevailed, and the Americans turned back to the town. They mounted a ridge beyond the center of Concord and then retreated to another which almost faced the North Bridge.

Colonel Smith put out his light infantry to dislodge them, but before they made contact the Americans crossed the North Bridge and climbed a hill near the farm of Major John Buttrick. Other militia companies were coming in now from nearby towns, and the number on the hill was about 400. Smith and Major Pitcairn mounted a slope in the center of town where the old burying ground still lies, surveying the countryside through telescopes. Wherever they looked the fields and hills were dotted with Americans hurrying to join the muster on the west side of the Concord River. Each man carried his flintlock, and at his belt were a bullet pouch and powder horn. It was not a reassuring sight to Smith and Pitcairn.

Smith ordered one company of light infantry to secure the South Bridge against the gathering storm of militia and minutemen. To the North Bridge, behind which the force seemed to be converging, he sent three companies and four more to cross the bridge and search the farm of Colonel Barrett farther west, where Dr. Church had reported that a large number of the stores were hidden.

Meanwhile, the grenadiers were poking around the houses and shops in town. Dr. Church's list proved of little value because of the weekend movement of the stores. The soldiers found some barrels of flour and some musket balls which they tossed into the millpond. They uncovered the wooden carriages of a few cannon which they set afire before Concord town house. This started a blaze in the building itself, but at the angry protests the troops extinguished it. At the South Bridge the soldiers had also found some wooden gun carriages which they burned.

Smoke rose over Concord. The militiamen had no means of knowing what was happening but feared the worst. "Will you let them burn the town down?" cried Joseph Hosmer, adjutant of the Concord companies, and his words resolved them into immediate action. They formed their companies in two ranks and marched down the hill. The road did not meet the bridge directly but turned toward it at a distance of about seventy-five yards. Captain Walter

Laurie, the British commander at the bridge, was dismayed by the size of the American force and sent a messenger back to Smith for reinforcements. He pulled back his men, some of whom he had deployed on the west side of the bridge, and tried to form a defensive stance.

The Americans came on, drums beating, fifes shrilling the stirring music of *The White Cockade*. Laurie's men fired a few desultory shots which fell harmlessly in the river. Then a full volley was directed at the Americans. Two were killed, two others wounded. John Buttrick at the head of the column turned and cried, "Fire, fellow soldiers! For God's sake, fire!" The British had begun it.

It was a long column, but as many militiamen as could get a clear shot fired at the British. Two privates were killed, a sergeant and eight men were wounded. Four of the eight officers in the defending British force were wounded. Laurie ordered an immediate withdrawal since the Americans were coming on strongly. He had no way of helping his wounded who hobbled back as best they could. On the road they met a force of grenadiers led by Colonel Smith who, being a fat, heavy man, had not speeded the arrival of the relief. There was nothing more to be done at the bridge. They went back to the center of Concord with their wounded.

Smith commandeered horses and chaises from the stables to carry the wounded back to Boston and made preparations to depart. It had not been a successful expedition. His men had found so few of the stores that he had accomplished little of the purpose for which Gage had sent him. Nevertheless, he had done what he could. His men were tired. They had been up since the middle of the previous evening, had marched something like twenty miles under heavy packs and they still had to get themselves to Boston on foot.

The fight at the North Bridge took place about ten o'clock. The company at the South Bridge, which had encountered no resistance, came in not long after, and about eleven o'clock the four companies were back from Colonel Barrett's farm without much to report in the way of unearthing stores. For almost an hour Smith rested his troops. Then he formed them in a column, put out the light-infantry companies as flankers on the east side of the road, and set the men in motion.

They proceeded without incident to Meriam's Corner, where the road turns sharply eastward toward Lexington. Militia companies which had been too late for the action at the North Bridge were coming in now, and at this time some 1,700 armed Americans may have been in the vicinity. Beyond Meriam's

Corner about a hundred feet there was a narrow bridge over the millbrook. As the last of the grenadier companies crossed the bridge the men turned and fired a senseless volley toward the farm buildings at the corner where some Reading companies were taking cover. The shots were too high to hit anyone, but this was the signal for battle.

The Reading men came toward the road and fired down on the redcoats. On the south, other arriving companies of militia and minutemen joined the attack from the other side. There was no order in this action. No one was in command. These were farmers shooting as individuals. Their only incentive was their fiery resentment against what they called the "parliamentary army" which had come out to challenge their liberties as British subjects. Their fire was probably not very accurate. But they were shooting into a massed column of soldiers, and it was almost impossible that they would fail to inflict casualties.

The stretch from Meriam's Corner to Charlestown is now known as "the Battle Road." You should drive it slowly and with many stops to read the markers which record the sharp and bloody actions of that long afternoon. On the Americans' part it was guerrilla warfare, for they were not fighting as organized units. They fired from behind trees, stone walls, boulders. The grenadiers attempted to return the fire, but as the Americans kept running ahead to new places of concealment the British soldiers had little chance of making an aimed shot. The light-infantry companies were more successful. Many of the American casualties were inflicted when the flankers shot and bayoneted the minutemen from the rear as they waited for the grenadiers to march past.

As the miles dragged under their boots and the farmers' shots thudded among them the discipline of the British column was lost. Colonel Smith was wounded in the leg. Major Pitcairn was thrown from his horse, which bolted, so that he continued the rest of the day on foot. At first the British picked up their wounded and tried to carry them. But after a time this became an insupportable burden. The grenadiers who had been shot straggled off the road where they were often treated tenderly after the shooting was over by a farmer's wife. But most of the wounds were fatal and after a few hours or a day or two the soldiers died and were buried near the scene of their fall. The sites of these burials, most of which are known, have been marked.

The troops were so exhausted by their extensive marches and the attack of the Americans that the expedition became a rout. As they neared Lexington the militia company of John Parker was waiting on a height and poured fire into their ranks in revenge for the volleys of the morning. By this time Colonel Smith was truly desperate. He had sent his express rider to General Gage around three in the morning, asking for reinforcements when he found that the countryside was aroused. No rescuing party had appeared, and his ammunition was almost gone.

The delay was not entirely Gage's fault, although when anything goes wrong in a military operation it is the commander's responsibility. Evidently Gage became increasingly worried after Earl Percy brought him the news that the expedition and its objective were public property. At four in the morning, long before he received Smith's express rider, Gage sent an order to Percy to alert the first brigade immediately and lead the troops over the Neck to meet Smith's force somewhere on the Concord road.

Through a series of blunders Percy did not receive the order until four hours later. Then he burst into action, and the foot soldiers were paraded smartly. But the marines who were part of the thousand-man force did not appear, and it was discovered that their order had been addressed to Major Pitcairn at his quarters. Of course Pitcairn had gone out the night before with the expeditionary force. At last the full brigade was mustered and marched over the Neck through Roxbury and Brookline to what was called the Great Bridge over the Charles River into Cambridge. Percy was thirty-three at the time, already an excellent and experienced officer. He was the eldest son of the Duke of Northumberland and, at his father's death in 1786, he succeeded to the ducal title.

As he approached Lexington about three in the afternoon he heard firing up ahead. He established headquarters in the Munroe Tavern east of the Green and spread his troops on both sides of the road to receive the exhausted and harassed regulars. He had brought two small field pieces which were useful in awing the Americans for a time. The six-pounders inflicted no casualties, though one shot put a hole through the meeting house beside the Green.

Percy rested the exhausted troops for half an hour, then got them up. He put companies of his fresh force in the van and at the rear, and they took the road to Charlestown. From there Percy planned to ferry them to Boston, avoiding the longer route through Cambridge and over the Neck. The troops were fired on all the way, and there was nothing much Percy could do about it except occasionally to halt the column and fire his six-pounders. Until they crossed Charlestown Neck they were targets of the Americans. It was dusk now and the end of an inglorious day for the British. Earl Percy arranged with the selectmen of Charlestown for a cease-fire until his men could be rowed across the Charles River to Boston. The regulars were at last free of the galling fire which had crashed among the men of the expeditionary force for the eight hours since they left Concord at noon and among Percy's rescuing troops for the five hours since they reached Lexington.

Gage's "secret" marchout had been a disaster almost from the beginning. The troops had failed in their primary mission to destroy the stores the Americans were stockpiling in and around Concord. There had been the dramatic encounter at the North Bridge which at the time seemed of no great importance to Smith. But then there was the unexpected and incredible attack of the Americans on his troops after they started for Boston. At this far distance the impetuosity and determination of the provincials still gives rise to wonder.

What drove them to begin and continue their attack? In a historian's analysis it was the fierce resentment against English troops threatening English subjects on English soil. For the Americans were as much English subjects as the soldiers and proud of their birthright. The soil was certainly English, and there was no thought of revolution. There was no thought of starting a war. But the Americans were jealous of their liberties and refused to accept Parliament's claimed power to send soldiers to coerce them. Americans had always governed themselves. They would die to keep this right. As nearly as anyone can analyze it now, that is why the Americans fought.

The casualty figures for the day are notable though not impressive considering the number of shots that must have been exchanged that afternoon. Of the British, 73 were killed, 174 wounded and evacuated to Boston, 26 missing, and most of these dead from wounds, a total of 273. Of the Americans, 49 were killed, 41 wounded, and five were missing.

Although the countryside was not largely populated, about 3,700 provincials took part in the action that day against a maximum British force (after Percy arrived in Lexington) of 1,800. Of course not all 3,700 of the Americans were present at any one time—probably not as many as half, spread out along both sides of the road. A minuteman stayed in the field as long as his powder and musket balls held out. Then many left since there was no way of getting fresh ammunition. But when dusk and night fell at Charlestown militia companies from as far away as New Hampshire and Connecticut were still arriving.

The warning net of the provincials had proved very efficient. These new troops and much of the force that had seen action all day were directed to Cambridge, where they became the nucleus of the Continental Army of which General George Washington took command on July 3, 1775.

With the establishment of an army in Cambridge the siege of Boston began. Now the colonial army had a purpose: to drive the hated redcoats out of the provincial capital and restore its government to the Americans. It took eleven months, but on March 17, 1776, the British transports and men-of-war left Boston harbor, never to return. With them they took 1,100 American Tories whose refusal to join the patriots made them forever hateful to those who would finally create a new nation on what Parliament in the end was forced to agree had ceased to be English soil.

After the United States signed the peace treaty with Great Britain in 1783 in Paris and cut itself off from the mother country, its early years were not placid. No sudden upsurge of prosperity lifted the infant nation. Instead, New England was plunged into the depths of a depression. The federal currency was wildly unstable and depreciated. Taxes were heavy, and now the Americans could no longer blame Parliament. It was their own leaders who were forced to impose the levies.

In addition, for the first time in our history what was then called "factionalism" arose. Before the break there were the Whigs, who were the patriots, and the Tories, who accepted British rule unquestioningly. But the Whigs were united in their principles, as the Tories were in theirs. There were no splinter groups among the Whigs, as there were none among the Tories. When the Tories sailed away on March 17, 1776, only the Whigs were left, and there were no differences among them. After the Declaration of Independence they were united in the decision to free the country from British rule by war.

When it was over, and the war was won, there began to be splits. For the first time political parties developed in America. During the long sessions of the Constitutional Convention in 1787 there were Federalists and Democrats who represented different ideas of how the new nation should be governed. There was bitter feuding between the two parties, familiar to us in our day, but new in the late eighteenth century. That the Constitution was adopted at all seems now almost a miracle, though a wonderful miracle which has stood for almost two centuries as the canon of our law.

Well, this is all political and prelude to the nineteenth-century flowering of New England in thought and word. It was quite a long time coming—after Massachusetts had regained its summertime of prosperity, after the War of 1812 when the nation was going ahead, and after the growth years of the 1820s. It had to wait for the coming to maturity of a new generation in the 1830s and 1840s. Now the nation that was already two centuries removed from its colonial beginnings had time to think about ideas which were not political. It had leisure to look beyond itself. There was suddenly a tremendous surge for knowledge. Whisperings of science were in the air, and who except a specialist knew about science? But people who were not specialists wanted to know and to read.

Out of this urge developed a profession that was new to America: Book-publishing firms began to appear in Boston. Of course books had been produced before but you might say they were "printed" rather than "published", for they were usually produced by printers like Edes and Gill in Boston, the firm that edited the fiery *Boston Gazette*. In the years leading up to the break with Britain they were glad to print a book, too, if there was money to pay for it. But there were no publishers who made a business of finding authors with manuscripts the public might want to read. In the 1830s such far-seeing gentlemen appeared and set up offices. There were none in Concord, but Boston was only a short distance away.

A book publisher could not prosper without authors, but all of a sudden there were authors in plenty and a public eager to read them. Oh, there were no best-sellers in the hundreds of thousands of copies we know today. But there was a book-buying public big enough to turn a tidy profit for the publisher and bring a nice income to the author.

Why did it happen just then? This is one of those mysteries no one will ever solve. It could not have happened in 1800, in 1815, in 1825. There were no American writers then. It happened in London in the late sixteenth century when Shakespeare and other men wrote their marvelous plays, and great poetry was thrust into the hands of those who could read. When Cromwell and his Puritans were thrown out it happened again in England, in the theatre, in poetry, in short bursts of greatness which came and subsided through the eighteenth century. But it had never happened in America until the 1830s. No one thought of writing as a profession.

Nathaniel Hawthorne thought of it when he was at Bowdoin College and while still a student he wrote a novel, published later but to no acclaim. After graduation, first in Salem, in Concord at the Old Manse, and then again in Salem he wrote constantly, but it was not until 1850 when *The Scarlet Letter* appeared that he achieved fame. But the profession of the man of letters was taking stature. Men kept journals to which they contributed their daily thoughts, and many of these were later published. In Concord Ralph Waldo Emerson became a lofty figure of thought with his books, his essays, his poetry. Bronson Alcott's journals were published, Henry David Thoreau's writings appeared, as did the poems of William Ellery Channing and others to bring the town into prominence as a center of the new literary flowering.

In Boston it was paced by Henry Wadsworth Longfellow, James Russell Lowell, and John Greenleaf Whittier, whose fire caught the imagination of the intellectual community. Writing became an excitement. When the New Year of 1840 dawned the Lowell Institute was inaugurated, and its series of lectures attracted turn-away crowds to the Odeon Theater, which seated 2,000. The first course was a group of twelve hour-long lectures on geology by Professor Benjamin Silliman of Yale. They were such sell-outs that they had to be repeated on subsequent afternoons, also to capacity audiences. It seems doubtful that lectures on geology would attract a general audience today. They did then. There was a hunger for knowledge of every sort. The Lowell Lectures were planned to meet this need with solid information. John Amory Lowell, the first trustee entrusted with the choice of subject and speaker, refused to engage men who might be fine orators—and oratory was greatly prized at this time—but who had no real instruction to give.

A case in point was that of William Makepeace Thackeray, the famed English novelist, who came to America on a speaking tour in the autumn of 1852. His ship docked in Boston—many did in those days—and he was lionized by the town. James Russell Lowell was a fellow passenger, and the two had become great friends, so he was introduced to Boston under the best of auspices. Thackeray was a giant of a man, about six feet four, and a genial one. Many expected John Lowell to tap him for the Institute, but Lowell was cautious. He probably had no doubt of Thackeray's capacity to be entertaining, but entertainment alone was not what he wanted. Except that he was a marvelous novelist, Thackeray was not an expert in any field. On his American lecture tour his subject was most often the "four Georges," who had reigned in Britain from 1714 until Victoria's time. But there was nothing particularly deep or revealing about the monarchs that Thackeray had to offer, and he was not invited to grace the Institute platform. In any case, it was not the sort of subject, conveying useful information, that Lowell thought proper.

With the literary renaissance, the lecturer came into his own. Any city of size and importance had its "lyceum," or course of lectures given by a series of eminent speakers. Concord had its own, and Emerson was active in its guidance. Emerson spent a good bit of his time as a lecturer, and it is said he was the first man who ever spanned the country to speak in San Francisco. If so, it must have been after 1869 when the last links of the trans-continental railway were spliced with a golden spike. The ride must have been an exhausting one, and I have no idea how long the journey from Boston may have been. George Pullman invented the sleeping car in 1867 and organized the Pullman Palace Car Company. But whether there were sleepers on the trains Emerson rode seems questionable. Still, he was a hardy soul, even in his seventies, and perhaps did not mind the discomfort.

Looking back, Emerson was the most important man who emerged during the literary renaissance in either Boston or Concord. He had more influence on the thought of this nation and abroad than any other American. His books were widely published in England and, in translation, found their way into the libraries of most foreign countries. Emerson was a Transcendentalist, a word adopted from the German eighteenth-century philosopher, Emmanuel Kant. In Boston a transcendental club was formed. But the movement in this country never had any exact philosophy. In simple terms it was devoted to inspiring the new believer to build on the old and press the mind farther to find new harmony, new horizons. It never advocated discarding the old, and so a great deal of puritanism was still carried in the new philosophy. It decreed only that man's mind was capable of reaching new heights of thought from which it could reach out to new truths.

In his life and writings, Emerson lived this philosophy. He was a calm, serene man, sure of what he believed and happy to teach it to others, but he was never doctrinaire or authoritarian. He was a quiet man, and when he spoke it was gently, not to gather apostles but simply to impress them with what he believed to be truth. He encouraged them to expand their minds.

Bronson Alcott, who kept a school for young children in Boston till he was discredited because he refused to discipline them physically, wrote this: "The true teacher defends his pupils against his own personal influence. He inspires self-distrust. He guides their eyes from himself to the spirit that quickens them.

He will have no disciple." This was the very essence of Emerson's teaching in his essay on *Self-Reliance*.

This was where the nation stood, fifty years and more after April 19, 1775. It had grown great, without forgetting its past. It had grown to a maturity which astonished even itself as it reached for new knowledge avidly. It was also conquering the land. The Louisiana Purchase, opening of the Northwest Territory—the nation was reaching out. But back in Lexington, Concord, and Boston, the things of the spirit were still dominant. Although men took up farmsteads farther west, the eyes of those at home were still fixed on thoughts that would be eternal. That is the way New England was reborn.

THE PLATES

Lexington

MUNROE TAVERN—LEXINGTON

As the grenadier and light-infantry companies reached Lexington in the pre-dawn hours of April 19, 1775, almost the first building they passed was the Munroe Tavern which stands on a slight eminence overlooking the road. The tavern must have been dark at that hour, for the proprietor, Sergeant William Munroe, was at Lexington Green. He had been ordered by Captain John Parker, captain of the militia company, to form the men on the Green. The tavern was built in 1698, a friendly, cozy inn and much frequented by those who lived at the east of the town.

That same afternoon when Earl Percy led out the first brigade to rescue the 800-man force of Colonel Smith he made the tavern his headquarters. Some of his troops raided the larder and the bar and shot an old man as he tried to leave the building. It was not a creditable performance by Percy's troops, nor was the firing of several buildings in the vicinity, though this may have seemed necessary to the commander to keep them from concealing the aggressive Americans. In any case, he was not here long before he started the British column on the long march back to Charlestown.

During the war Sergeant Munroe rose to the rank of colonel and returned to his tavern when hostilities were over. Here he entertained General Washington at dinner in 1789. This room and others are pleasantly furnished with contemporary pieces, and this is the first place you will visit when you drive out from Boston.

32

MASON HOUSE—LEXINGTON

Across the road from the Munroe Tavern is this pleasant white clapboard house which is the oldest in Lexington. It was begun in 1680 after John Mason moved from Watertown to establish a new residence at a time when there was much interest in setting up a village for the community. When the act of incorporation was adopted in March, 1712, John Mason was elected one of the two constables. Our photograph shows the central portion with a suggestion of the wing at the right. The house is set back from the road with a gracious lawn in front. It is privately owned and not open to the public but well worth stopping your car on the road to enjoy the façade of this colonial veteran.

When Earl Percy's men met the troops who had marched from Concord the regulars went on a rampage of destruction and plundering of the houses in the vicinity. In addition to the few that were burned, others suffered vandalism and thievery. Whether the culprits were from Percy's command or the returning Concord expedition is hard to establish, but it seems plausible that they were Percy's, who were comparatively fresh. The total damage in Lexington has been summed up as £1,761 2s. 3d. The Mason House suffered with the others. This is a black mark against Percy—if he knew of it. A commander is expected to control his men.

BUCKMAN TAVERN—LEXINGTON

This pleasant inn was the mustering point for the militia in the early hours of Wednesday, April 19. After Paul Revere and William Dawes arrived at the house of the Reverend Jonas Clarke with their report that the British regulars were coming out to seize Concord's military stores, John Parker gave the order for the bell in the old belfry to ring out the alarm. Within a few minutes the members of the militia began coming in, trailing their flintlocks. Messengers were sent down the road toward Boston to see if they could catch sight of the troops. All of them were captured by Gage's officer patrols and did not return. With no news it was decided that the Lexington company should not expose itself and be "discovered" by the British if they indeed marched past. Parker dismissed the men but warned them to be ready to reassemble at the beating of the drum. Some went home; most remained.

At four-thirty Thaddeus Bowman, last of the Lexington scouts sent down the Boston road, galloped back with news that the British were only a half mile away. Parker aroused young William Diamond and told him to beat the drum. Then he ordered Sergeant Munroe to form the men on the Green. What had happened in the intervening hours to change the earlier decision not to show themselves has never come to light. No contemporary document mentions it. The militiamen formed two ranks, muskets loaded and primed. There they stood when the British marched up and there these farmers made history.

OLD BELFRY—LEXINGTON

On a hill near the Green stands a replica of the Old Belfry which rang out the alarm to the militia in the early hours of April 19, 1775. It was originally erected on this site, but seven years before the battle it was moved to the Green where it stood when the call to assemble was sounded. In 1909 it was blown down by a gale, and then an exact duplicate was erected on the original hill. Lexington had long had its bell, but there was grumbling that it could not be heard at any far distance. In 1761 a Lexington man, Isaac Stone, presented the town with a fine new bell weighing 463 pounds which was gratefully accepted at town meeting. It was this bell that pealed the alarm.

The belfry escaped damage by the British at the time a shot from one of Earl Percy's small field pieces put a hole through the meeting house. But over the years it had fallen into decay, which was responsible for its collapse in the 1909 storm. The replica was sturdily constructed on its hilltop and dedicated in 1910.

HANCOCK-CLARKE HOUSE—LEXINGTON

A short distance from the Green you will come upon this ancient dwelling. It is now named jointly for the two pastors who served the people of Lexington for over a century, since each occupied this parsonage for more than fifty years. The house was built in 1698, the year the Reverend John Hancock began his ministry. After his death in 1752 it was three years before the town fathers agreed on a successor. Then they chose the Reverend Jonas Clarke in 1755, and he remained pastor until his death in 1805. The original house was much smaller and was enlarged in 1734 to its present dimensions.

Mr. Hancock served in more quiet times, but during the brewing quarrel with England Mr. Clarke became Lexington's leader in both intellectual and political thought. He was a dedicated patriot from the first, and his hand drafted the official papers the town sent to the General Court in Boston, protesting the oppressive acts of Parliament.

It was here that a younger John Hancock—he was thirty-eight that year—and Samuel Adams were staying when Paul Revere brought the news that the regulars were coming out. Hancock was for taking his place with the militia, but Adams dissuaded him, pointing out that they had a different service to perform for the cause. They were due in Philadelphia on May 1 when the Second Continental Congress would convene, of which Hancock was president.

The Hancock-Clarke house is open to the public and a visit will leave you with a vivid recollection of history lingering in your mind.

MINUTEMAN STATUE—LEXINGTON

At the eastern point of the Green stands this bronze statue of a minuteman, looking down the road in the direction from which the British troops would appear. It is generally thought of as the figure of John Parker, captain of the militia company, done by Henry Hudson Kitson. If so, it is not portraiture, for there is no likeness of Parker on which it could have been modeled. And Parker would have been somewhat older than the face suggests, for he was a veteran of the French and Indian War, and that took place nearly twenty years before. Nevertheless, it is a handsome and stirring monument with the minuteman standing erect, flintlock ready to guard the rights of Lexington.

Parker survived the day of April 19 but he was grievously wounded at the Battle of Bunker Hill on June 17. He was taken to Boston by the British, where he died a few days later as a prisoner of war.

The mounting of the figure is particularly right, for the man stands on a mound of boulders taken from the stone walls behind which the Americans fought that day. As the photograph shows, they are not assembled in any formal pattern but just as the walls were built and still are in New England. This monument is worth much more than a glance. As you stand before it you can feel swelling up the emotion of that early morning. No one knew what it would bring. But whatever happened the farmers would be ready. They were standing erect and facing the east.

42

THE OLD BURYING GROUND—LEXINGTON

The first stone is dated 1690, and most of them are slate, as are those in the foreground. Slate was the usual material used for tombstones in colonial times because it was more easily worked than the granite which came later. Wandering through an ancient cemetery and reading the inscriptions is something to evoke a sense of the age of our country and a memory of the illustrious as well as the simple dead whose deeds wrote the early history. You will find here the single grave of the Reverend John Hancock and the Reverend Jonas Clarke, for they were buried together, and that of the sturdy Captain Parker whose militia company fired the first American shots of the Revolution.

In colonial times it was sometimes the custom to carve rather humorous inscriptions on tombstones, for death seemed an inevitable fact of life. I do not remember any in this burying ground, but I have read many in other old cemeteries. One that I recall, though I do not remember where it stands, reads this way: "Beneath this stone and bit of clay lies Uncle Peter Daniels, who early in the month of May took off his winter flannels." The rhyme is not perfect but good enough as seventeenth-century rhyming went, and Daniels may well have been pronounced "Dannls" at the time. You may puzzle over why a bereaved family would choose such sentiments for a tombstone. I have always thought it was done with tender affection for one much loved and remembered fondly not as a saint but as an erring though practical earthly soul.

44

THE BATTLE GREEN—LEXINGTON

This boulder marks the line of the Americans on the morning of April 19. It is inscribed with the words Captain Parker is said to have spoken as instructions to the militia company before the British came up: "Stand your ground. Don't fire unless fired upon. But if they mean to have a war let it begin here." There is no contemporary record of Parker's having said these words. They were recalled by a veteran in 1825, fifty years after the event, and they are fine words. The first two sentences are quite believable. They are what we know Parker said. The third seems far more doubtful. There was no thought on either side that morning of a civil war starting, and it would have been a civil war between Englishmen. The Americans were mustering in Lexington to uphold their liberties as English subjects. The British were marching to deprive the provincials of the munitions they had gathered in Concord to oppose any attempt to coerce them. It would be fifteen months before the reality of revolution took hold at the meetings of the Continental Congress in Philadelphia.

Across the Green stands the First Parish Church, not a witness of the battle in 1775. At that time the meeting house was at the Green itself and its location is marked. The present church with its ascending spire is a fine colonial piece of architecture which fits into the history of this ancient town.

HARRINGTON HOUSE—LEXINGTON

This handsome colonial house beside the Green with a fine pediment over the doorway looks as fresh today as it must have in the moonlight when Jonathan Harrington, Jr., left it for a rendezvous with death. He would have leaped from his bed at the post-midnight clanging of the alarm bell, pulled on his clothes, said goodbye to his wife and, going downstairs, picked up his bullet pouch, his powder horn, and flintlock. Then he would have headed for the Buckman Tavern.

He probably stayed there until the dawn muster. This must have been a time of tense inner excitement, and it seems incredible that any man thought sleep possible. Then at first light when word came that the British were hardly half a mile away the men of the militia company went out into the fragrant morning and assembled on the Green. Captain Parker ordered them to load and prime.

There they stood waiting, a company of soldiers ready for what might come. Jonathan Harrington stood with them, his musket in his hands. He was cut down by a bullet in the first British volley. Mortally wounded, he dragged himself to his house. His wife had been watching from the window and went to meet him. He died at her feet on the doorstep.

48

MARRETT AND NATHAN MUNROE HOUSE— LEXINGTON

This house, built in 1729, lies across the triangular Green from the Harrington house. Both are privately owned and not open to the public. Marrett Munroe's name does not appear on the roster of the Lexington militia company, though he served in the army later. He was a prominent citizen of the town and elected selectman for several years in the 1760s.

Nathan Munroe was a member of the militia company that faced the British on April 19. When the order came to disperse he jumped a wall beyond the Green, then turned and fired at the British, though this was after their volleys were directed at the Americans. He records this in a deposition taken in December, 1824, almost fifty years after the battle, when the Americans were still trying to impress history with the fact they had not forced the battle by shooting first.

Nathan went with the company on June 17–18 and must have taken part in the Battle of Bunker Hill, where Captain Parker was critically wounded. Most of the men who built and defended the redoubt which the British attacked on Breed's Hill—in front of Bunker Hill—were part of the militia companies stationed at Cambridge. From the recorded dates of June 17–18, however, it would seem that the Lexington company had been alerted that morning, marched to Cambridge and then on to Breed's Hill. There would have been plenty of time, for the battle did not begin until afternoon.

PATRIOTS' DAY—LEXINGTON

In 1894 April 19 was established through an act of the Massachusetts legislature as Patriots' Day and a legal holiday throughout the state, as is June 17, Bunker Hill Day. The first celebration was a notable one, attended by the governor and lieutenant governor and other state officials. There were a procession, a band concert, "literary exercises," and a ball at night. Since that time a modern Paul Revere has ridden over the old route and clattered into Lexington to warn the town that "the regulars are coming out." While the news is received with somewhat less alarm than it was in 1775, companies dressed in replicas of Revolutionary uniforms assemble from Lexington and nearby towns, and there is a great parade. The photograph shows the "ancient and honorables" greeting express-rider Revere in the background, and the parade will soon begin.

While this is a local celebration, if you could be there on that day it would take your memory back two centuries. The resplendent uniforms were not there when the militia company paraded in 1775. The provincials simply wore what they always wore. But you cannot escape a quickening of emotion, a sense of pride, that on this very road the British marched—on this very Green the Americans stood. Now history and reality merge in your mind. In 1775 what happened was indeed reality.

Concord

MERIAM'S CORNER—CONCORD

When the British light infantry and grenadiers reached this point they executed a smart "Column Right," for here the road turns north toward Concord. Meriam's Corner is named for Joseph Meriam, one of the original settlers, and his descendants. Here was the ample Meriam farm and it was just east of here that the militia and minutemen, marching down the Lexington road with fife and drums playing sighted the approaching troops and turned back to the town.

The English soldiers had no cause to notice the farm but they would have reason to remember it in the early afternoon as they started back to Boston. It was here that the Americans who had taken cover behind the farm buildings began the spontaneous fire on the British column. What started it was that the last of the grenadiers suddenly turned and loosed a volley at the farm buildings. It is not even certain that they saw the provincials, for they had given no other fire since leaving the center of Concord. In any case the militia and minutemen were outraged and rushed to the road which lies just beyond the bottom of our photograph. They shot into the column and began an attack which would never stop for all the miles of that long afternoon.

HILL BURYING GROUND—CONCORD

This cemetery, the oldest in Concord, rises up an eastward slope in the center of the town. While there were undoubtedly earlier burials, the oldest stone that remains is that of Joseph Meriam, who died in 1677. It is a short, chunky stone of Welsh slate. This stands up better than native slate which is more brittle and susceptible to chipping and deterioration. The Welsh slate was imported from North Wales and was undoubtedly expensive. In the early days it would also have been difficult to transport the twenty miles from Boston's wharves.

When the British troops marched into the town they were halted in the road while Colonel Smith and Major Pitcairn mounted the slope of the burying ground. From there they had a clear view to the southwest, west, and northwest and could see the Americans hurrying to join the muster near Major Buttrick's farm beyond the North Bridge. When they descended to the road Smith gave his orders for deploying companies of light infantry to the South Bridge, the North Bridge, and to search the farm of Colonel James Barrett. After that he sent the grenadiers to go over the houses in the town for stores Gage had told him were hidden there.

WRIGHT TAVERN—CONCORD

As the Buckman Tavern in Lexington was designated as the mustering point for the militia, so the Wright Tavern, built in 1747, served the same purpose in Concord. When Dr. Samuel Prescott brought the news of the marchout of British regulars, the guard at the town house immediately rang out the alarm. The first man to report, he recalled, was the Reverend William Emerson, though he lived at some distance in the Old Manse near the North Bridge. Soon the pleasant bar of the tavern was filled with militia and minutemen. For a time they discussed what to do, but since it would be several hours before the expeditionary force could arrive the men returned to the task of further concealing the stores in the town. A little later one dedicated woman brought in the communion silver from the church and sank it in a barrel of soft soap. It was quite safe there but so blackened by the action of the lye when it was rescued next day that it required a silversmith to burnish it before it could be used.

After the British arrived the officers used the tavern as a headquarters, being careful to pay for any food and drink they consumed. There is a legend, first recorded by Lemuel Shattuck in his history some sixty years later, that Major Pitcairn ordered a glass of brandy "and stirred it with his bloody finger, remarking, 'He hoped he should stir the Yankee blood so before night.'" One of the younger officers may have made such a boast, but it seems highly unlikely that Pitcairn would have uttered these words. He was an older man and not given to heroics.

NORTH BRIDGE—CONCORD

Our photograph shows the modern replica of the Old North Bridge where the engagement between the Americans and the British took place. It was dedicated in 1956. The structure is sturdily built and its supports retain the rustic appearance which the first bridge presented. The view is taken from the western side of the Concord River where the Americans approached. In the distance is the monument, erected in 1836 to commemorate the battle, when Ralph Waldo Emerson's *Concord Hymn* was first sung with the well-remembered line, "By the rude bridge that arched the flood."

There was no bridge at all at the time of the ceremony. Emerson's poem takes note of this: "Time the ruined bridge has swept down the dark stream." The selectmen decided in 1793 to abandon the roads on the west side of the river which led to the North Bridge. A new structure was built farther north called Flint's Bridge. Some time after that the original North Bridge fell into the river.

Ebenezer Howard left money for a new bridge, and this was built in 1875 so the minuteman monument could be placed on the west or American side of the river. This bridge had cedar railings and small summerhouses to make it picturesque but it was declared unsafe in 1888. In 1909 a cement replica was constructed. For a time automobile traffic was permitted, but the road commissioners feared the bridge was not strong enough for cars and this was stopped. No automobiles are permitted on the present structure.

THE MINUTEMAN—CONCORD

This is another view of the North Bridge from the western side with Daniel Chester French's statue of the Minuteman in the foreground. French lived in Concord at the time and, though he was not yet twenty-five, he was commissioned by the town to do this monument for the centennial celebration on April 19, 1875. The plow on which his left hand rests is symbolic, for a minuteman was expected to leave whatever he was doing instantly in case of an alarm and hurry to join his company. Of course none of the Lexington or Concord minutemen left their plowing in the morning of April 19 for the alarm came not long after midnight.

This is the first of many fine sculptures that French executed. He was born in 1850 and lived until 1931. His master work is the seated Lincoln in the Lincoln Memorial in Washington. It was unveiled in 1922 and has inspired millions of visitors to feel in this brooding marble figure a sense of the spiritual quality of the martyred President. Had he never done anything else, however, the Minuteman would have proved the stature of French as a sculptor. It evokes an emotional memory of the battle that took place on the April morning with the British on the far side and the Americans approaching the bridge, determined to drive the redcoats out.

THE OBELISK, NORTH BRIDGE—CONCORD

This is where the British stood on the morning of April 19, three light-infantry companies numbering about a hundred men. From here they fired on the provincials marching toward them from the other side and, in turn, took the Americans' fire before retreating. The grave of two British soldiers killed here is marked. The obelisk was dedicated at an April 19 ceremony in 1836.

This entire area of the North Bridge and its surrounding land consisting of 155 acres was acquired some years ago by the National Park Service and constituted one of two parts of the Minute Man National Historical Park. The other and much larger section, comprising 557 acres, covers a stretch of about four miles of the Battle Road running from Meriam's Corner to Lexington, where the heavy fighting began shortly after noon on April 19. These acquisitions, authorized by Congress, follow recommendations of the Boston National Historic Sites Commission designed to preserve old treasures from demolition.

It is planned to keep the rural appearance of the North Bridge area, not much changed, except for the monuments, from the way it looked on the morning long ago. There is a spacious parking lot across Monument Street which runs out from Concord, but no cars are permitted to enter the short stretch of road which approaches the bridge.

THE OLD MANSE—CONCORD

While this mellow house is now more than two centuries old, it was young when the battle was fought. The Reverend William Emerson, grandfather of Ralph Waldo Emerson and minister of the Concord church, built it in 1765. That it is always called "the Old Manse" derives from the title of a popular book which Nathaniel Hawthorne wrote when he lived here from 1842 to 1845, *Mosses from an Old Manse*. The house faces Monument Street but it is set in the middle of a large field which runs along the eastern approach to North Bridge. An opening has been made in the stone wall there, and a path leads directly to the house.

William Emerson was a fiery patriot like most of the pastors of the meeting houses in Boston and the surrounding countryside. He had served as chaplain of the two Provincial Congresses convened in the local meeting house, and his sermons were often more political in theme than strictly religious. He turned out with his musket at the alarm bell in the early morning of April 19 and recorded the time in his diary as between one and two o'clock. He took part in all the maneuvers of the militia and minutemen that morning until they crossed North Bridge. Then he went over the field to protect his wife and children and give such comfort as he could to a growing group of frightened parishioners. He stayed with them outside the Manse, keeping an eye on the British soldiers. He was there until after the battle and the regulars marched away—up Monument Street to the center of town.

BULLET HOLE HOUSE—CONCORD

Although it has had many additions and alterations, this still has title to being the oldest house in Concord for the original building, still a part, was put up in 1644. It stands on the east side of Monument Street, almost opposite the Old Manse, and had a fine well of fresh water which the British soldiers stationed at the bridge came back frequently to enjoy.

Elisha Jones, his wife, and two small daughters went into the cellar and stayed there until they heard the firing at the bridge. Then Elisha had to see what was going on. He went up the stairs, his family following, to the second floor. The British, retreating from the bridge, were marching down Monument Street. Jones raised a window and poked out his musket, but his wife made him pull it back, fearful that this hostile gesture might cause the British to burn the house down. Elisha agreed but descended the stairs and stood in the open door of his shed. A light infantryman in the rear of the column saw him and aimed a shot. It struck within three feet of Jones' head, good shooting for a musket of those days.

For many years the bullet hole was covered by glass to mark the scar. Some time ago this identification was removed because the family was bothered by so many visitors coming to see it. The house is privately owned and not open to the public. But it is still known in Concord as "the bullet hole house."

68

REUBEN BROWN HOUSE—CONCORD

Reuben Brown was a saddler with a shop where he had been busy all autumn and winter making cartridge boxes, belts, and other military gear for the minutemen. Some time after Dr. Prescott brought in the news that the British were approaching Lexington the Concord men sent Brown on horseback to find out whether the regulars really came out. Some were skeptical and they wanted first-hand news from a man they trusted. Brown clattered off and was in time to observe the firing on Lexington Green from a distance. When he returned he was asked, "Were the British firing ball?" He replied that he did not know but "thought it probable," the understatement of the day with dead and wounded men stretched out on the Green.

Reuben Brown rejoined his company. When the British arrived and the grenadiers began their search his shop caught fire but the soldiers extinguished the blaze before much damage was done. It is interesting to note that, in contrast to their later vandalism in Lexington, the British troops in Concord were quite correct in their deportment. They did not loot, they were gentle with the housewives, saying they had not come to destroy private property but only the provincial stores. It was a very orderly occupation.

LEXINGTON ROAD—CONCORD

Once you are in Concord proper the past enfolds you for there is a sense of repose in the houses and the great trees which shade them. This view is taken from somewhere near Monument Square, looking along the Lexington Road. There is harmony in the houses on this street, some of them already standing when the British marched past in 1775. But whether they were or not, the general style of architecture which began about the 1740s and 1750s lingered for nearly a hundred years. There were no grand houses in the Concord of that day, for there were no great fortunes here. But the dwellings, to use a New England word, were "comfortable," which means they were ample and pleasant, quite adequate for the generous families that grew up in their gracious rooms. Wood was the material of most, though the second house in the photograph has brick ends.

Monument Square, just behind our camera, was the exact center of the six-mile-square tract which was granted by the General Court in 1635 to the settlers, and it was here that the village was begun. The public buildings—the town house and the meeting house—were established here when the town was young. Somewhere near here you should park your car and explore the scene on foot to absorb the atmosphere of what is still a fine colonial town.

72

FIRST PARISH CHURCH—CONCORD

In 1900 the venerable meeting house, built in 1712, which housed the two Provincial Congresses in 1774 and 1775, burned down, the fate of so many wooden structures. In 1901 this fine building rose on the site. Its style is not colonial but Greek Revival with a columned portico and a Grecian pediment above the doorway. Surmounting it is not the spire that adorns most New England meeting houses but a bell tower. Still, it does not disturb the harmony of Concord's architecture and is a handsome building to carry on the tradition of worship in this ancient town.

The old meeting house which it replaced was a much sterner building, an oblong box as were most of them. The term "meeting house" lingered on from the first days of this country to distinguish the more simple houses of worship from the Anglican churches, but "church" gradually acquired stature as a proper word for the Congregational meeting houses, too. In those days there was no central organization of the Congregational faith. When a new community was established the town fathers set out to find a man who could serve as pastor. He need not have had divinity schooling, and there were few enough in the colonies who had received this training. It was his dedication and the quality of his sermons that were important. When he was found a meeting house was erected and a congregation "gathered" (what a nice, descriptive word it is!), and then there was happiness in the town.

THE COLONIAL INN—CONCORD

Part of this long building at what is known as the "Crossroads" was a repository of colonial stores in 1775, not only munitions but barrels of food stuffs. There is no record that the grenadiers explored it. If they did, the supplies had been removed and concealed elsewhere. Originally this was a series of separate buildings and the central portion was at one time a general store. Many years ago the buildings were connected and turned into an inn. Before this happened Henry David Thoreau lived for a time in quarters to the right.

The inn is near Monument Square and is a pleasant, comfortable place for the visitor and his family to enjoy a meal of New England cooking, though the menu is by no means confined to New England dishes. It is a rambling structure of many rooms, as the exterior implies, but despite its practical arrangements for meals the interior retains a sense of age that is a welcome feeling when you are relaxing in this old town.

ANTIQUARIAN HOUSE—CONCORD

This is the headquarters of the Concord Antiquarian Society, which took it over in 1886. The house was here in 1775 and it is now a treasury of Concord relics and rooms that illustrate the successive periods of the town's history from the seventeenth century on. There are frequent daily tours during which the rooms and their furnishings are explained, and to join one of these will leave you with a record of how our ancestors developed from simple beginnings to a state of chaste elegance as the years flowed along. One of the points of interest is an exact reproduction of the library of Ralph Waldo Emerson with the furniture, the books, and other mementoes of the great man.

Among other relics is one of the two lanterns which were hung in the steeple of the Old North Church on the evening of April 18 to signal the watchers on the Charlestown shore that the British were coming out over the Back Bay. The surprising thing is that it was lit by only a single candle. It was a good thing that the night was clear or the twin beams of the two lanterns could never have been seen across the Charles River. There are other relics, of course, and there is a fine diorama of the fight at the North Bridge which will bring it to life in your mind.

RALPH WALDO EMERSON HOUSE—CONCORD

The house was bought by Emerson in 1835. He enlarged it and put in trees and other planting that give it the mellow appearance it shows today. It is a rather simple, square house really, certainly not a showy one, but there is an air of solidity about it that reflects the taste of its owner as it reflects the air of Concord itself. Emerson was born in Boston in 1803 but he knew Concord well and had spent some time at the Old Manse which his grandfather built as pastor of the Concord church. Emerson's father was also a minister, pastor of the First Church in Boston, and from boyhood the young Emerson was pointed toward the same career. In 1829 he was ordained and made minister of the Second Church in Boston, whose congregation was Unitarian. Almost from the beginning, it seems, he felt cramped in the churchly life. He was restless and wanted to let his mind soar and find new truths instead of dealing with old ones. He resigned in 1832 to take up the career of a lecturer and man of letters.

The rooms of the house reflect his search. After he gave up his pulpit he went abroad and in England became the friend and companion of Thomas Carlyle, William Wordsworth, and Samuel Taylor Coleridge. His conversations with the three men did much to shape and firm the new philosophy that Emerson had begun to develop.

After he moved into this house he became very much the citizen of Concord, walking the fields or the streets, attending town meeting, devoting himself to the Lyceum and other civic activities. He was highly respected in the town and deeply loved.

SLEEPY HOLLOW CEMETERY—CONCORD

The land which for many years had been known as Sleepy Hollow was bought by the town in 1856 to be used as a cemetery. It contains the graves of most of the illustrious men and women who made Concord a center of the nineteenth-century literary renaissance. It is a lovely, peaceful place today, and nothing has been done to disturb the gentle contours the land has always shown. One woman who played here as a little girl before it became a cemetery described it as "a long ridge of low hills covered with pines, where violets and anemones abounded in the spring, where birds and squirrels made merry in their season, and where children ran wild on Saturday afternoons winter and summer." What a pleasant picture!

The transformation of Sleepy Hollow into a cemetery did not alter any of the natural beauties and pleasures. Birds still sing, squirrels play, wildflowers grow in spring beneath the pines. The graves of great literary figures who lie here, while not grouped together, are in more or less the same vicinity. They were all friends in life; it seems only proper that they should be within calling distance in death. Here is Ralph Waldo Emerson, who spoke at the cemetery's dedication in 1856. Here is Henry David Thoreau, one of Emerson's closest companions, as was Bronson Alcott, who lies nearby with his extensive family including, of course, Louisa May, the famed author of *Little Women*. Nathaniel Hawthorne chose to rest here, too. There are others, but these names are enough to show you that when you walk through the cemetery you are in the shadow of greatness.

82

THE WAYSIDE—CONCORD

Nathaniel Hawthorne bought this house on the Lexington Road in 1852, but in 1853, when Franklin Pierce became President, he offered him the consulship in Liverpool, which Hawthorne gratefully accepted, for he was eager to visit England and Europe. The family lived in Liverpool till 1857, then went to Italy where they spent two years in Rome and Florence. In 1860 they came back to Concord and moved into The Wayside.

Hawthorne was born in Salem in 1804, and went to Bowdoin College where he was a classmate of Henry Wadsworth Longfellow. Franklin Pierce was a class ahead of them, but these three developed a lifelong friendship. When Hawthorne returned to Salem after graduation his early fiction was published in magazines and collected in book form. It was favorably reviewed, but there was little money in it. Then, in 1850 *The Scarlet Letter* appeared and was a huge success. A year later *The House of Seven Gables* was published, and Hawthorne's money troubles were over.

When the seven-year absence was over Hawthorne's health was noticeably failing. He wrote constantly, as he always had, but the old magic had gone. He was bothered by the stream of visitors and had a cupola built on top of the house where he could work in seclusion. In 1864 he set out with his wife for Maine. In Plymouth, New Hampshire, he was stricken and died.

Our photograph shows The Wayside when it was undergoing a renovation. This has long since been completed, and the house is restored to its former pleasant appearance.

84

ORCHARD HOUSE—CONCORD

A visit to this house on the Lexington Road is one of the most rewarding Concord has to offer. It was the home of the Bronson Alcott family from 1848 to 1882 and enshrines many girlhood pleasures which Louisa May Alcott brought to life in *Little Women*, published in 1868 and 1869. The book was an instant success, both popularly and financially. Louisa rescued the family from debt and, with her later books, continued to keep it solvent.

From 1842 to 1845 the Alcotts lived next door in The Hillside, which Nathaniel Hawthorne later bought and renamed The Wayside. In *Little Women* Louisa fictionalized the adventures that she and her three sisters enjoyed, partly from the Hillside days and partly from Orchard House. If you have younger children, and particularly girls, wandering through the rooms of Orchard House provides a rich experience they will never forget.

This was an ancient farmhouse and so rundown when they bought it that many people felt it was "only good for firewood." But Bronson Alcott showed a surprising turn for architecture and designed its renovation. His wife and the girls turned enthusiastically to refurbishing the interior. They papered and painted the rooms. May, the youngest daughter, who was a natural artist, added her touches here and there. When it was all shipshape in July, 1848, friends who had called the house hopeless came to admire it.

There it stands now, open to the public, much as it was when it was lived in by "the little women."

SCHOOL OF PHILOSOPHY—CONCORD

This small chapel was built on the grounds of Orchard House under a canopy of pines. It opened on July 15, 1879, when Bronson Alcott was eighty, and courses continued until his death in 1888. Louisa wrote in her diary the day the school opened, "Father has his dream realized at last, and is in his glory with plenty of talk to swim in." A month later the *Journal* has this entry: "The town swarms with budding philosophers, and they roost on our steps like hens waiting for corn." News of the school must have spread afar, for Louisa also wrote, "People will enjoy something new in this dull old town, and the fresh Westerners will show them that all the culture in the world is not in Concord." Lectures were given by a series of men including Emerson and, of course, Alcott himself. The final session in 1888 was a memorial service for Alcott.

Bronson Alcott was one of the important figures in the nineteenth-century flowering of New England. He was a pure idealist; impractical, certainly improvident, for none of his concerns led to making money. His two great experiments in what he called "consocial living," Fruitlands, at Harvard, Massachusetts, and Brook Farm, were failures, yet he was widely known and respected by the intellectual community. He was one of the founders of the Transcendental movement, whose motives were vague but chiefly concerned in impressing men with the doctrine of stretching their minds toward a more perfect personal realization of the meaning of life.

GRAPEVINE COTTAGE—CONCORD

While Concord is famous for the Battle and for its towering literary figures, Ephraim Wales Bull contributed to its fame in quite another field: He originated and perfected the Concord grape. He was born in Boston in a house with a large garden and from early boyhood was fascinated by growing things and their cultivation. At the age of eleven he was apprenticed to a gold-beater, a man who pounds sheets of gold into gold leaf. In 1836 he showed traces of lung trouble, and his doctor advised him to leave Boston. He went to Concord where he bought this small cottage and some adjoining land for a shop.

His heart was in the land, and eventually he abandoned gold-beating for farming. His great passion was the cultivation of grapes. He was determined to grow a better table grape than any on the market. In 1849 he had a beauty which he tested for three years and then exhibited before the Massachusetts Horticultural Society, where its size and flavor created a sensation. In 1854 the Concord was put on the market in Boston and earned its originator $3,200 the first year. In a short time it was being grown by nurserymen everywhere, and Bull's proprietary rights slipped from his hands.

The following year Bull was elected to the Massachusetts legislature and in 1856 to the state senate. He read papers and lectured widely, a short stocky man with a long flowing beard. His success with the Concord continued to stimulate him to experiment with other seedlings. He died in 1875 and is buried in Sleepy Hollow Cemetery, another illustrious name to be added to Concord's great.

WALDEN POND—CONCORD

This pleasant sheet of inland water near Concord is sacred to the memory of Henry David Thoreau. He lived there for two years from 1845 to 1847 in a small cabin he built himself, sparsely furnished and with few visitors. He was a rarity of the literary renaissance, a naturalist and, in modern days, we would call him a "loner". He lived his life in the out-of-doors, but his thoughts were bubbling within himself, confided to his massive *Journals*. He was born in 1817 and graduated from Harvard with the class of 1837. After that he came back to Concord.

He was a strange and rather wonderful man. He never married. When he needed money—and he needed little—he hired himself out to a farmer for a time or practised surveying, at which he was expert. But his primary interest was the study of nature. He had no desire to acquire wealth. Ralph Waldo Emerson was his great friend, and Thoreau occupied his house when Emerson went abroad in 1847. His chief study was always the fields, the forests, the streams. His books are dedicated to that, particularly *Walden*, the record of his happy life at the pond. He was an intuitive woodsman, though never a killer of wild things, and took pleasure to be at the paddle of a canoe, which he handled with the effortless skill of an Indian.

Today Walden Pond is not a clutter of summer cottages as so many New England lakes are. The prospect of its wooded shores is not much different from the one Thoreau knew well over a hundred years ago. For one so active in the open air, it is strange to recall that Thoreau contracted tuberculosis and died in 1862 at the age of fifty-five. He is buried with the immortals in Sleepy Hollow.

PATRIOTS' DAY PARADE—LEXINGTON

Here we are back in Lexington viewing the annual celebration of April 19. The marshals, the color guard, the drums and fifes, the bands give a note of majesty to a day which had anything but majesty in 1775. But that was two hundred years ago, and Lexington has a right to celebrate it in grander dress today. Not only the Lexington company, but others from nearby towns come to join the parade, and that is right for so it was in 1775. Every town in the countryside was aroused to oppose the British regulars.

In 1775 the militia had no such uniforms as these. The men were farmers and they answered the call in farmers' rough clothes. But it is pleasant to think that in these parades the men honor our forefathers with formal military dress their ancestors would have been proud to wear that fateful morning on the Green.

It is a state-wide holiday in Massachusetts, and in the foreground you see the backs of schoolchildren out to watch and applaud. "Here they come!" They have been coming each April 19 since 1894 when Patriots' Day was officially declared by the legislature. They are marching to the memory of a drum which beat out the call to assemble in the early dawn of long ago. This day Lexington hears its echo, loud and clear.